STAR WARS
THE
MANDALORIAN

The Mandalorian, a legendary bounty hunter, has been tasked
with returning a foundling known as Grogu to his kind, the Jedi.
But evil Imperial Moff Gideon has other plans for the tiny being and will do
anything in his power to seize him back and exploit his incredible and mysterious abilities.

Join Mando and Grogu on their journey as they travel
across space in the second season of the hit Disney+ show. Uncover the story of each
hero and villain, learn about the amazing creatures, and get behind-the-scenes peeks from
a galaxy far, far away.

TITAN EDITORIAL
Editor Jonathan Wilkins
Group Editor Jake Devine
Art Director Oz Browne
Editorial Assistant Calum Collins
Production Controller Kelly Fenlon
Production Controller Caterina Falqui
Production Manager Jackie Flook
Sales and Circulation Manager
Steve Tothill
Marketing Coordinator Lauren Noding
Publicist Phoebe Trillo
Digital and Marketing Manager
Jo Teather
Acquisitions Editor Duncan Baizley
Publishing Directors Ricky Claydon
& John Dziewiatkowski
Operations Director Leigh Baulch
Publishers Vivian Cheung &
Nick Landau

DISTRIBUTION
U.S. Newsstand Total Publisher Services, Inc.
John Dziewiatkowski, 630-851-7683
U.S. Distribution Ingrams Periodicals, Curtis
Circulation Company
U.K. Newsstand Marketforce, 0203 787 919
U.S./U.K. Direct Sales Market: Diamond Comic
Distributors
For more info on advertising contact
adinfo@titanemail.com
Contents © 2022 Lucasfilm Ltd. &
All Rights Reserved
First edition May 2022
*Star Wars: The Mandalorian: Guide to Season
Two* is published by Titan Magazines, a division
of Titan Publishing Group Limited, 144
Southwark Street, London SE1 0UP
Printed and bound in china
For sale in the U.S., Canada,
U.K., and Eire

ISBN: 9781787738676

Titan Authorized User. TMN 4156

LUCASFILM EDITORIAL
Senior Editor Robert Simpson
Creative Director Michael Siglain
Art Director Troy Alders
Asset Management Bryce Pinkos,
Chris Argyropoulos, Erik Sanchez,
Gabrielle Levenson, Jason Schultz,
Sarah Williams

Story Group Leland Chee, Pablo Hidlago,
Matt Martin
Creative Art Manager Phil Szostak

Special Thanks: Tracy Cannobbio,
Christopher Troise, Kevin Pearl,
Shiho Tilley, Eugene Paraszczuk,
Dave Filoni and Jon Favreau

DISNEY EDITORIAL
Editorial Director: Bianca Coletti
Editorial Team: Guido Frazzini (Director,
Comics),Stefano Ambrosio (Executive
Editor, New IP),Carlotta Quattrocolo
(Executive Editor, Franchise),
Camilla Vedove (Senior Manager, Editorial
Development), Behnoosh Khalili (Senior
Editor),Julie Dorris (Senior Editor), Mina
Riazi (Assistant Editor), Gabriela Capasso
(Assistant Editor)

Design: Enrico Soave (Senior Designer)
Art: Ken Shue (VP, Global Art),
Roberto Santillo (Creative Director),
Marco Ghiglione (Creative Manager),
Manny Mederos (Creative Manager),
Stefano Attardi (Illustration Manager)
Portfolio Management: Olivia Ciancarelli
(Director)
Business & Marketing: Mariantonietta
Galla (Senior Manager, Franchise), Virpi
Korhonen (Editorial Manager)
Text: Alessandro Ferrari, Silvia Dell'Amore
Photography: Francois Duhamel, Justin
Lubin
Graphic Design: Falcinelli & Co. / Mauro
Abbattista
Pre-Press: Lito milano srl

CONTENTS

SEASON TWO
EPISODE
GUIDE

In season one, covering chapters 1 through 8, a few years after the rise of the New Republic, a bounty hunter known as the Mandalorian is hired to deliver a mysterious asset to a client who works for evil Imperial Moff Gideon. However, upon discovering that the bounty is a Force-sensitive infant, the Mandalorian decides to rescue the asset, risking his own life and reputation. After countless adventures, the Mandalorian sets off on a journey to reunite the Child with his kind. But Moff Gideon has other plans for the tiny being…

1 / Previous Spread:
The Mandalorian and
the Child explore the
barren lands of the
planet Corvus. Concept
art by Brian Matyas.

2 / A ferocious krayt
dragon emerges from
the sands of Tatooine.
Concept art by Doug
Chiang.

3 / The ice spiders
attack the *Razor Crest*.
Concept art by Ryan
Church.

CHAPTER 9: **THE MARSHAL**

Din Djarin is on the look-out for fellow Mandalorians who could help him return the Child to his kind. On a seamy planet, he meets with gangster Gor Koresh, who points him to the old mining settlement of Mos Pelgo on Tatooine. Once there, Mando meets local marshal Cobb Vanth, who wears Mandalorian armor bought from Jawas. Upon learning that a huge krayt dragon frequently attacks Mos Pelgo, Mando offers to help in exchange for the marshal's armor. Together with Vanth, the town's villagers and a clan of Tusken Raiders, the bounty hunter manages to kill the krayt dragon. He then leaves Tatooine with the Child and the reclaimed armor.

CHAPTER 10: **THE PASSENGER**

In return for hints about where to find a Mandalorian covert, Djarin agrees to take a frog lady and her unhatched eggs to Trask, an estuary moon in the Kol Iben system, to reunite with her husband. As the eggs are very delicate, Mando, the Child and their passenger must travel sublight and risk being noticed by other ships. Indeed, they are soon approached by two New Republic X-wing fighters. Trying to elude them, Mando and the others end up on a nearby icy planet. There they are attacked by hundreds of white ice spiders, but, at the last minute, the X-wing pilots step in and help them fight back. Finally safe, Mando, the Child and the Frog Lady resume their journey to Trask.

CHAPTER 11: **THE HEIRESS**

On Trask, Mando enters a local inn seeking information. A Quarren sailor offers to take him by boat to fellow Mandalorians, who allegedly are a few hours away. Aboard the vessel, Mando and the Child are attacked by a group of fishermen who want Djarin's beskar, but are suddenly helped by three Mandalorians. The warriors, led by Bo-Katan Kryze, are on a mission to retrieve weapons from an Imperial Gozanti freighter, and they ask for Mando's help. The Mandalorians manage to take control of the ship and seize the gear. In return for Djarin's help, Bo-Katan Kryze tells him to find Ahsoka Tano on the planet Corvus.

4 / Mandalorian Bo-Katan Kryze and her allies fly to the rescue of Djarin and the Child. Concept art by Brian Matyas.

4 /

5 /

CHAPTER 12: **THE SIEGE**

Before heading to Corvus, Mando decides to stop on Nevarro to have his ship repaired. There he and the Child reunite with Greef Karga and Cara Dune, who have cleaned up the town as the new magistrate and marshal. Karga and Dune enlist Mando to take down an old Imperial base. Once there, they realize that the base is actually a laboratory where Dr. Pershing has been conducting trials with the Child's blood and that Moff Gideon is still alive. The old friends manage to destroy the base. They part ways, and Mando is finally ready to leave for Corvus.

5 / Thanks to Greef Karga and Cara Dune, Nevarro has become a far more respectable place. Concept art by Ryan Church.

ALZMANN

CHAPTER 13: **THE JEDI**

On Corvus, Mando heads to the city of Calodan to find Ahsoka Tano. The planet's magistrate, Morgan Elsbeth, hires him to kill Tano and offers a beskar spear as payment. In the woods, Mando finds Ahsoka, who immediately notices the Child. Through the Force, Tano learns that the Child's name is Grogu and that he was trained by the Jedi until the rise of the Empire. She then agrees to train him in exchange for Mando's help in fighting the magistrate. The two manage to defeat Elsbeth and free the city, but Ahsoka Tano realizes that she cannot train Grogu due to his attachment to the Mandalorian. However, she tells Djarin to take Grogu to the temple ruins on Tython, where he may choose his path.

7 /

6 / Former Jedi Ahsoka Tano fights Morgan Elsbeth's scout guards on the planet Corvus. Concept art by Brian Matyas.

CHAPTER 14: **THE TRAGEDY**

Once at the temple ruins on Tython, Djarin places Grogu on the seeing stone at the top of a mountain, where Grogu soon enters into a meditative state. Meanwhile, Mando is approached by a man called Boba Fett and Fennec Shand, who was saved by Boba and is now in his service. Boba Fett explains that Cobb Vanth's armor was his father's and he wants it back. In exchange, he promises to ensure Grogu's safety. Suddenly, the group is attacked by Moff Gideon's stormtroopers and dark troopers, who kidnap Grogu and flee while Gideon destroys the *Razor Crest*. Fett and Shand take Mando to Cara Dune, whom he asks for help in springing former Imperial Migs Mayfeld from a New Republic prison.

7 / The dark troopers kidnap Grogu at the temple ruins on Tython. Concept art by Christian Alzmann and Erik Tiemens.

CHAPTER 15: **THE BELIEVER**

As Nevarro's marshal, Cara Dune has Mayfeld remanded to her custody. She then takes him to Mando, Fennec and Boba, who want Mayfeld to get the coordinates for Moff Gideon's cruiser. As he needs access to an Imperial terminal, Mayfeld suggests going to a secret mining hub on Morak. There Mando and Mayfeld manage to enter the facility disguised as drivers. Inside the hub, Mando has to take his helmet off in order for the terminal to scan his face and grant him access. Just as he locates Gideon, Valin Hess, Mayfeld's former officer, approaches him. Mayfeld blasts Hess and shoots his way out with Djarin. Finally safe on Fett's ship, Mando sends a message to Moff Gideon and tells him he's coming to rescue Grogu.

8 / Migs Mayfeld and
Mando take control of
an Imperial Juggernaut
on Morak. Concept art
by Brian Matyas.

8 /

CHAPTER 16: **THE RESCUE**

Mando asks Bo-Katan and Koska Reeves, her ally, to help him rescue Grogu. Kryze agrees to help in exchange for Gideon's cruiser and the Darksaber. She then sets up a plan, thanks to which Djarin and the others successfully assault the Moff's ship. While Dune, Shand, Kryze and Reeves fight the guards, Mando heads to Grogu. He is confronted by the dark troopers but manages to throw them out of the ship. Then he faces Moff Gideon and defeats him, thus becoming the Darksaber's new owner. The dark troopers fly back inside and prepare to attack but are suddenly wiped out by Jedi Master Luke Skywalker, who sensed Grogu's presence through the Force and has been searching for him. With a heavy heart, Mando parts ways with Grogu and promises that they will meet again.◗

9 / Contrary to what Mando thinks, there is something on Morak: a secret Imperial mining hub. Concept art by Anton Grandert.

THE MANDALORIAN

A glint of his beskar armor is enough to send shivers down the spines of his opponents, but ever since the Child has been in his care, the Mandalorian has also displayed a softer paternal side. Despite his strong affection for the kid, the bounty hunter is determined to reunite him with his own kind – and, most importantly, to keep him out of the Empire's sight.

FRIENDS WILL BE FRIENDS

While searching the galaxy for Grogu's home, Din Djarin has made numerous enemies – from mercenaries to magistrates, Imperials and, of course, droids. Yet he's also managed to make a few friends, such as former Guild agent Greef Karga and Galactic Civil War veteran Cara Dune.

Once a wary lone wolf, the bounty hunter has come to realize he can sometimes afford to trust others. At times, he has even asked some acquaintances to keep an eye on Grogu when he's been out on risky business (though he very much prefers to take Grogu wherever he goes). On Trask, when Bo-Katan Kryze and her clan made him agree to help them steal weapons from an Imperial freighter, Mando left Grogu with the Frog Lady – whom he had earlier helped reunite with her husband – something that he probably wouldn't have done before.

1 / By creed, the Mandalorian must look after Grogu until he is of age or reunited with the Jedi.

2 / Greef Karga and Cara Dune greet Mando and Grogu upon their return to Nevarro.

2 /

3 /

3 / Mando doesn't approve of Bo-Katan Kryze's code of conduct.

4 / Unlike Mando and his former tribe, Bo-Katan Kryze and her Mandalorian allies are comfortable removing their helmets.

Despite this slight change of attitude, Din Djarin is still the deadly and calculating warrior the Outer Rim has come to know, not afraid to pull the trigger if anyone stands in his way or, even worse, tries to harm Grogu.

THESE ARE THE WAYS

Because of his past as a foundling, Djarin is very devoted to Mandalorians and his former tribe's precepts, known as the Way of the Mandalore,

which he strives to follow to the letter. However, he seemed to be unaware that other tribes and clans do not necessarily adhere to the same code of conduct.

When he first met Bo-Katan Kryze and her companions, Djarin noticed that they were comfortable taking their helmets off – a practice, as far as he knows, strictly forbidden by his people – and accused them of not being real Mandalorians. From that statement, Bo-Katan understood that Djarin is a member of the Children of the Watch, a specific

4 /

Mandalorian cult whose aim is to restore "the ancient way" – that is, a more conservative approach to life.

Initially upset, Mando has gradually come to understand that things aren't always black and white, especially when, as Migs Mayfeld would say, "things get messy" and one has to cross one's own lines. Nevertheless, the bounty hunter still firmly believes that "there is only one way: the Way of the Mandalore."

FOUNDLING FATHER

Though entirely different in many ways, Grogu and Mando both had quite a difficult start in life. Just like Grogu, Djarin was rescued at a tender age by a Mandalorian warrior – a mutual experience that allowed the bounty hunter to quickly empathize with him.

At first, when taking Grogu in, Mando was merely adhering to his tribe's precepts, according to which foundlings must be taken care of until they are of age or reunited with their kind. However, what started as a mere task undertaken "by creed" quickly became something more.

5 / Mando and Grogu have formed a "father-son" relationship.

6 /

On their journey together, the bounty hunter has grown attached to Grogu and often acts as a fatherly figure – like when he tells him to mind his manners or not play with his food! He is also aware of the little one's "powers" – though he's not entirely sure what they are – and often encourages him to experiment with his abilities.

The emotional bond formed with Grogu has profoundly changed Mando's perspective on things. To save the little one, he even goes so far as to break his creed's rules on more than one occasion – like when he took off his helmet in order to get Gideon's ship coordinates.

7 /

6 / Before parting ways with Grogu, Djarin removes his helmet so Grogu can see his face.

7 / As Grogu doesn't talk yet, he cannot communicate verbally with Mando. However, thanks to their bond, the two always find a way to understand each other.

NEW GEAR

When the *Razor Crest* was destroyed by Moff Gideon's light cruiser, the Mandalorian lost the majority of his equipment. Yet he can still count on his sturdy armor as well as on two great new weapons.

In the city of Calodan on the planet Corvus, Mando obtained a spear of pure beskar – one of the few metals that can withstand lightsaber blows. The spear is so tough that it even survived the destruction of Djarin's ship... and the strength of a dark trooper.

Having defeated Moff Gideon in a duel, Djarin has also become the owner of the Darksaber, an ancient black-bladed lightsaber that can cut through anything but beskar.

8 / Just like his new staff, Mando's armor, too, is made of beskar.

9 / Though he didn't mean to, by defeating Moff Gideon, Djarin has become the rightful wielder of the Darksaber, the legendary weapon Bo-Katan Kryze is after.

8 /

9 /

BEHIND THE SCENES

Season 2's storyline allowed actor Pedro Pascal to physically embody Din Djarin much more. Unfortunately, spending more time on set didn't make his performance any easier. Indeed, Pascal still had to portray a character who is "armored from the tips of his toes to the top of his head," thus having to convey emotions in a subtle and economical way.

While shooting the second season, Pascal particularly enjoyed working with actress Amy Sedaris, who portrays sabacc player Peli Motto, the operator of hangar 3-5. Pascal said of her "Somebody who makes you spit-laugh right into your helmet will always be my favorite thing."

As his face is always concealed, Pascal is rarely recognized by children as the actor who plays the main character in *The Mandalorian*. "I always feel bad," he said. "I don't have the Child with me; I'm not wearing a helmet. And they look, and they're like, 'Who's this guy?'"

11 /

12 /

10 / Executive producer Dave Filoni on set while directing a scene from Chapter 13.

11 / Chapter 14 director Robert Rodriguez at work.

12 / Series creator and executive producer Jon Favreau directs actress Amy Sedaris in a scene from Chapter 9.

13 / Peli Motto, played by Amy Sedaris, and the Frog Lady, portrayed by Misty Rosas, shoot a night time scene.

14 / Mando carries his cargo – and little Grogu – while he goes to Mos Eisley on foot.

14 /

GROGU

The wide-eyed youngling known as the Child has found a way to reveal his name; yet very little is known about his species and homeland. Strong with the Force, tiny Grogu needs to be reunited with the Jedi; in the meantime, he better stay out of trouble – and keep his small hands off the *Razor Crest*'s control knob...

1 /

2 /

1 / Little Grogu always feels safe when held by Mando.

2 / Grogu's floating crib has saved his life on many occasions.

UNRAVELING THE PAST

As with most toddlers, Grogu still cannot talk, which obviously makes it difficult to gather any information about his past. Luckily, as a Force-sensitive being, he can communicate by mentally connecting with other Force wielders. This allowed former Jedi Ahsoka Tano, whom Grogu and Mando met on the planet Corvus, to delve into the little one's thoughts.

According to Ahsoka, the Child, whose real name is Grogu, was raised at the Jedi Temple on the planet Coruscant. There he was trained by several Jedi Masters until the end of the Clone Wars and the fall of the Jedi Order. When the newly formed Galactic Empire came to power, Grogu was taken away from the Temple and hidden from Imperials. To stay safe, he also had to conceal his Force-related abilities.

Grogu's memories of what came after are quite blurry. Still, Tano sensed the years that followed were lonely and sad ones for Grogu. Little did he know that, sometime later, a rough yet kindhearted bounty hunter would come to the rescue...

3 / Former Jedi Ahsoka Tano tests Grogu's Force-related abilities.

4 / The Child reaches out to the Force in the hope a Jedi may sense his presence and come searching for him.

5 / At school, Grogu is more interested in cookies than he is in the class.

6 / Grogu uses his powers to catch a stone, demonstrating he is still strong with the Force.

3 /

4 /

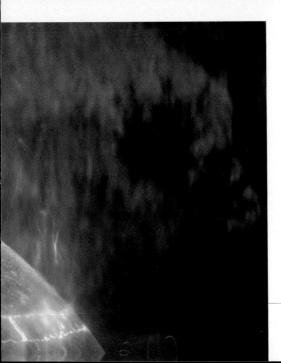

A VERY SPECIAL KID

Just like Yoda, a wise Jedi Master who belonged to the same species as him, little Grogu is quite strong with the Force.

From mudhorn lifting to wound healing, Grogu has employed his Force-related powers on several occasions. After Moff Gideon kidnapped him on Tython, little Grogu even managed to knock out two stormtroopers using the Force. Such efforts, however, are still quite intense for the youngling and require him to rest.

Though very skillful, Grogu had to suspend his Jedi training at the end of the Clone Wars, which means that he still has to fully master his abilities. Nonetheless, when it comes to obtaining what he wants – whether it's a cookie or his beloved control knob – Grogu wields the Force like a Jedi!

7 / Art by Brian Matyas

RETURN TO THE JEDI

8 / The Mandalorian and little Grogu bid farewell to Ahsoka Tano.

9 / Grogu has chosen to resume his Jedi training under the guidance of Luke Skywalker.

After noticing the strong bond between the bounty hunter and Grogu, Ahsoka Tano realized she couldn't train Grogu herself. As she further explained, Grogu's attachment to Mando "makes him vulnerable to his fears," something that no Jedi should ever risk.

After being taken to Tython and placed among the ruins of an ancient temple as suggested by Tano, Grogu made clear he wanted to resume his Jedi training. In fact, he reached out to other Jedi through the Force in the hope they would come for him.

Grogu's call was not in vain, for a legendary Jedi Master known as Luke Skywalker managed to track him down and offered to train him. However, before agreeing to follow him, Grogu asked, in his own cooing way, Mando's permission – a last demonstration of affection before going back to the way of the Jedi.

BEHIND THE SCENES

Based on Christian Alzmann's concept art and physically brought to life by special effects studio Legacy Effects, Grogu's main puppet took around three months to build.

Sound editors Matthew Wood and David Acord, who previously worked on the *Star Wars* sequel trilogy, took care of the vocals. Grogu's original sounds were obtained by recording a bat-eared fox and a kinkajou at a wildlife rescue near San Diego. As explained by Acord, these animals' noises proved to be particularly suitable for they had a "really cute, almost childlike quality to them."

But according to executive producer Jon Favreau, Grogu needed to be more "human-sounding and relatable." This was achieved by using real baby vocals for the moments where the youngling is most "talkative," while animal sounds were merely employed for his grunts and coos. The final touch was made by using a high-pitched version of Acord's own voice for particularly articulated vocalizations. ◗

10 / When it comes to round objects, Grogu cannot help the urge to take them – or eat them.

11 / Grogu uses the Force to steal cookies. Concept art by Christian Alzmann.

10 /

11 /

BO-KATAN KRYZE

A fierce Mandalorian warrior, Bo-Katan Kryze has only one purpose: to retake and rule Mandalore, her people's homeworld. In order to rightfully claim the throne, Bo-Katan Kryze must retrieve an ancient weapon that once belonged to her and is now in the hands of evil Moff Gideon…

SERVING A HIGHER PURPOSE

Contrary to some Mandalorians, including those who used to operate on Nevarro, Bo-Katan Kryze has no time to waste with bounties and assignments; in fact, she and her allies have more significant matters at hand.

Born on Mandalore, Bo-Katan of Clan Kryze fought the Empire in the so-called Great Purge, a conflict where the majority of her people were massacred. Forced to flee, Bo-Katan is now determined to retake her home planet and claim the throne.

As the experienced warrior she is, Kryze is well aware that such an ambitious endeavor requires a good array of weapons for the battles ahead – and all the help she can get. When she met Mando on the moon Trask, she didn't think twice and enlisted his help to steal a plethora of weapons from an Imperial Gozanti freighter, a mission they successfully accomplished. Impressed by his bravery, Kryze asked Djarin to join her and her allies, but he refused as he had to complete his own quest first.

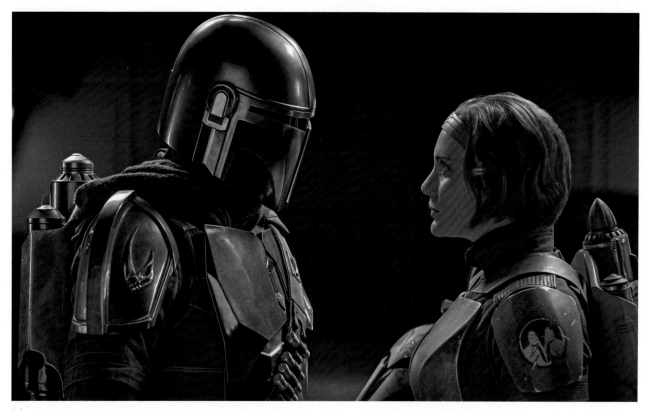

1 /

1 / In exchange for his help, Bo-Katan Kryze will help Mando find a Jedi.

2 / Born on Mandalore, Bo-Katan of Clan Kryze is the last of her line.

But standard weapons aren't enough. Whoever seeks to rightfully claim Mandalore's throne must be in possession of the Darksaber, a legendary weapon created by Mandalorian Tarre Vizsla. Kryze was the last Mandalorian to wield the Darksaber before Moff Gideon somehow took it away from her during the Great Purge.

Eager to seize the weapon back, Kryze agreed to help Mando rescue Grogu after he was kidnapped by the evil Moff. However, during a strenuous duel, Mando managed to disarm Gideon, thus becoming the rightful owner of the Darksaber as its lore dictates.

STRONGER TOGETHER

Despite her disapproval of the Children of the Watch's drastic doctrine, Kryze strongly believes that Mandalorians shouldn't fight against each other, because, as she said herself, they "are stronger together." Poised and disciplined, she doesn't care for useless quarrels, as she very much prefers to save her energy for real enemies.

Nevertheless, Kryze is a Mandalorian born and bred. As such she, too, believes there are boundaries no one should ever dare to cross, like wearing Mandalorian armor without being one. When she met bounty hunter Boba Fett – who indeed wears his father's Mandalorian armor – she disdained him as a fraud and called him "a disgrace." This, however, didn't blur her judgment when it came to cooperating with Boba for a greater good – fighting Moff Gideon.

3 / Mando and Boba Fett enlist Bo-Katan Kryze and her ally's help to rescue Grogu from Moff Gideon.

4 / Bo-Katan and her allies have but one purpose: retaking Mandalore.

5 / A seasoned warrior, Bo-Katan Kryze has great combat skills.

3 /

4 /

6 / Stronger together: the Mandalorians hijack an Imperial Gozanti freighter on Trask.

7 / Front of Bo-Katan
Kryze's blue-and-
gray armor

7 /

ARMOR AND WEAPONS

As Mandalorians' beliefs may differ, so does their armor, which has distinctive colors and markings depending on the owners' clans and cultures.

Bo-Katan's armor, painted blue and gray, has been passed down through generations. Like all Mandalorians, she wears a T-shaped visor helmet; however, unlike Mando's, Kryze's helmet is equipped with a range finder, a useful targeting device. Additionally, Kryze wears a cuirass, shoulder pauldrons, vambraces and gauntlets, whereas neither she nor her allies wear a cape.

In terms of weapons, Bo-Katan carries two blaster pistols, gauntlet blades, a grappling line and a jetpack – a rather broad collection, with just a single dark-bladed piece missing…

8 / A common feature in Mandalorian helmets, range finders are targeting devices that can be slid over visors to enhance vision.

9 / Mandalorian helmets have infrared scanners to detect the body heat of their targets.

8 /

9 /

BEHIND THE SCENES

Other than Dave Filoni, no one knows Bo-Katan Kryze better than Katee Sackhoff, the actress who voiced her in both the *Star Wars: The Clone Wars* and *Star Wars Rebels* animated series. Sackhoff loaned her voice to Bo-Katan for over ten years; yet she never really thought she might end up portraying her in a live-action series.

"Years ago, when she first started, I said, 'You never know: this works out, this could become live-action one day, and she was like, 'Okay, great, Dave. I'm sure,'" said executive producer Dave Filoni. "And so, when she showed up on set and she's wearing the full outfit, carrying her helmet, she just looked at me like, 'I can't believe you said this would happen, and

it's happening.' She's so great at playing these types of gunslinger characters and she is just Bo-Katan to me."

Perhaps surprisingly, knowing the character inside out didn't really help Sackhoff with her performance. The actress explained, "While it gave me a tremendous understanding of who she was as a person, it didn't help me to figure out her physicality. It didn't help me to figure out the way her face moved or the way she walked. I had seen the way she moved, but it was in animation. And so to translate that in a way that didn't look cartoonish was actually harder than I thought it would be."

Quite curiously, the name Bo-Katan hints at the cat of Filoni's wife, Anne. Her cat's nickname is boogie. "Boogie-cat-Anne" has thus become Bo-Katan. ◉

10 / Inside the Imperial freighter's cockpit, director Bryce Dallas Howard talks with the actors.

AHSOKA TANO

With her two lightsabers and strength in the Force, Ahsoka Tano seems like the Jedi Mando has been looking for. Brave and kindhearted, Ahsoka quickly empathizes with Grogu; yet she fears his attachment to Mando may take him down to a dark path...

THE NICE LADY

As her physical appearance suggests, Ahsoka Tano is a Togruta, a species characterized by facial markings, horn-shaped sensory organs known as montrals and three long tentacle-like head-tails called lekku.

Selfless and kind, Tano doesn't shy away from helping the oppressed and others in need. On the forest planet Corvus, she teamed up with the Mandalorian to free the city of Calodan and its citizens from the rule of ruthless magistrate Morgan Elsbeth.

Ahsoka's generosity doesn't prevent her from being a skilled and relentless fighter. Indeed, during a strenuous duel, she managed to defeat Elsbeth even though the latter wielded a spear made of pure beskar, notably one of the few metals lightsabers cannot cut through. Later, to reward him for his help, Tano offered the spear obtained from Elsbeth to Djarin, claiming that a beskar weapon "belongs with a Mandalorian."

1 /

1 / Behind her smile, Ahsoka bears the burden of a difficult past.

2 / Ahsoka Tano is determined to free Calodan's citizens from evil Morgan Elsbeth.

FEAR OF THE DARK

Formerly guardians of peace and justice in the Galactic Republic, Jedi are powerful knights able to tap into the energy field known as the Force. Hunted down by the Empire, the Jedi were ultimately destroyed at the end of the Clone Wars. The few who managed to survive were forced to scatter across the galaxy and hide out.

Ahsoka Tano was trained as a Jedi but eventually decided to leave the Order and follow her own path instead.

Ahsoka is profoundly strong in the Force and is experienced enough to wield it effectively. On the planet Corvus, she used the Force to mentally connect with Grogu and hear his thoughts, thus managing to delve into his memories and learn his name.

Because of her abilities and expertise, Mando believed that Tano could be the perfect mentor for Grogu, and asked her to train him. But upon noticing the strong bond between the two, Ahsoka refused, worrying Grogu's affection for the bounty hunter would make him "vulnerable to his fears." And fear, as wise Jedi Master Yoda once said, "leads to anger. Anger leads to hate" – feelings not even the most powerful Jedi of all time would be able to control.

3 /

4 /

3 / Thanks to the Force, Ahsoka Tano and Grogu can hear each other's thoughts.

4 / A skilful warrior, Ahsoka often wields two lightsabers at the same time.

5 / Ahsoka Tano's white blades highlight the fact she has no affiliation with the Jedi.

DOUBLE TROUBLE

Despite her departure from the Order, Ahsoka Tano still uses the weapon she learned to wield during her training: the lightsaber. More specifically, Ahsoka has not one but two lightsabers, which she generally uses simultaneously.

Probably the best ally of any Jedi, lightsabers are legendary weapons, more impressive when wielded by Force-sensitive beings. Their plasma blades are powered by specific crystals known as kyber crystals, which Jedi younglings must find as part of their training.

In terms of fighting style, Tano usually wields a standard-bladed lightsaber as her primary weapon and a shorter one – also known as a shoto lightsaber – as an off-hand weapon. She also often alternates between the standard grip and the so-called reverse grip, in which the lightsaber is held with the blade pointing down along the wielder's forearm.

6 /

BEHIND THE SCENES

7 /

Created by George Lucas and Dave Filoni, the character of Ahsoka Tano made her debut in the animated series *Star Wars: The Clone Wars*, where she was introduced as the Jedi Padawan of Anakin Skywalker.

A beloved character in both the *Star Wars: The Clone Wars* and *Star Wars Rebels* animated series, Ahsoka Tano appears in *The Mandalorian* from the second season only, a decision made by executive producer Dave Filoni.

"I intentionally didn't do anything with her in season one because I didn't wanna mess it up. It's a character that George and I created. She's one of the first things I ever drew for *Clone Wars*. People know this character: they've watched her grow up, and the challenge was to take all of the elements we had and evolve them into this live-action version."

A fan of *The Clone Wars* herself, actress Rosario Dawson started her preparation for the role by

6 / The thrilling duel between Magistrate Elsbeth and Ahsoka Tano.

7 / "This belongs with a Mandalorian". Ahsoka Tano hands Morgan Elsbeth's staff to Mando.

8 / Next Spread: Diana Lee Inosanto looks on as executive producer Dave Filoni directs Rosario Dawson.

rewatching the animated series as well as the whole saga. "It was really fun to see how Ahsoka's physicality changed, and her facial expressions changed, and her voice and her tenor changed as she just evolved."

Makeup-wise, bringing Tano physically to life proved quite challenging. As makeup designer Brian Sipe explained "Her character was tricky cause it was walking that line of finding her look between human-realistic and something that would satisfy the fans of the *Clone Wars* graphic image."

Another problem arose with Ahsoka's two lightsabers. According to property master Josh Roth, "With the batteries and with the receivers, all the different wireless gak we had to put inside of it, the saber kept getting bigger and bigger, and Dave was just 'No, it can't look like this.'" The problem was eventually solved by using an external battery so that the lightsabers could maintain their elegance and slenderness. ◗

BOBA FETT

Boba Fett may be "a simple man making his way through the galaxy," yet his past and story are anything but simple. After working for countless clients, including the Empire, the legendary bounty hunter is now after his own asset: his late father's Mandalorian armor.

LIKE FATHER, LIKE SON

Before he became, during the Imperial Era, one of the greatest bounty hunters in the galaxy, Boba Fett was just a devoted son – though, technically, he wasn't born from a mother and a father.

Boba Fett was, in fact, the pure genetic replica of Jango Fett, a bounty hunter who served as the original host for the creation of a secret army of clone troopers at the end of the Old Republic. The clones were engineered by Kaminoans, a species highly skilled in cloning techniques, and would later become the mighty army of the Galactic Republic.

On top of the payment received for being the clones' genetic source, Jango Fett had requested only one additional thing: a clone to raise as his own child – Boba Fett.

Contrary to the other units, who were genetically modified to be more docile and take orders without question, Boba Fett was an unaltered clone and, as such, he was better able to develop his own personality.

During his childhood on planet Kamino, Boba Fett formed a strong bond with his father and quickly unveiled a great talent for combat. In fact, he already knew how to use some of his father's weapons, such as his ship's blaster cannons, at a tender age.

At the beginning of the Clone Wars, in a conflict known as the Battle of Geonosis, Jango Fett was killed right in front of his son's eyes. This was the spark that led Boba Fett to become, years later, a ruthless mercenary feared across the whole galaxy.

1 / Miraculously, ruthless bounty hunter Boba Fett has managed to survive his encounter with the Sarlacc.

2 /

THE REVENANT

During the Imperial era, Boba Fett's reputation as a bounty hunter grew until he was regarded as the best in the business. Over the years, he worked for various clients from the criminal underworld – including Tatooine's crime lord Jabba the Hutt – as well as for the Dark Lord himself: Darth Vader. While his career progressed, Boba Fett started to wear Jango's Mandalorian armor and helmet.

In a fight against Jedi Master Luke Skywalker and his allies, Boba Fett was thrown inside the maw of the Sarlacc, a massive tentacled creature that swallowed the bounty hunter alive.

The legendary Boba Fett was left for dead inside the Sarlacc's stomach – but fate, as he said himself, "sometimes steps in to rescue the wretched."

Surprisingly, Boba Fett managed to get through the encounter, but his survival came at a price. The hunter lost his most precious belonging: his father's armor

2 / The scars on Boba's face are constant reminders of what he went through to survive.

3 / Even with no armor, Boba Fett is quite intimidating.

3 /

4 / Boba Fett shows off his armor and weaponry.

5 / Boba dusts off the wrist laser hidden in his left gauntlet.

5 /

ARMOR AND WEAPONS

Inherited from his father, Boba Fett's Mandalorian armor bears the marks of countless battles and enemies. Originally silver and blue, it was repainted with a new green-and-red color scheme. The armor consists of a helmet equipped with a range finder, breastplate, pauldrons, gauntlets and kneepads. During the Imperial era, Boba Fett would often adorn his armor with war trophies, such as braids from dead prey.

The bounty hunter can also count on a pretty diverse array of weaponry. Just like Mando's, Boba Fett's gauntlets are equipped with a flamethrower and a whipcord launcher, while his kneepads hide rocket dart launchers.

Of course, no Mandalorian armor would be complete without a jet pack and Boba Fett's is no exception. However, his device comes with an extra feature: an explosive rocket that the wielder can launch from it.

Boba Fett's arsenal of weapons further includes two weapons presumably obtained from Tatooine's Tusken Raiders: a cycler rifle and a club known as a gaffi stick.

4 /

6 /

6 / Boba wields a
gaffi stick presumably
obtained from Tusken
Raiders.

7 / At last, Boba Fett
has retrieved his most
precious belonging:
his late father's
Mandalorian armor.

8 / Next Spread: Boba
sits in the throne room
inside Jabba's Palace.

BEHIND THE SCENES

Boba Fett has always been director Robert Rodriguez's favorite character. "I was nine years old when the first *Star Wars* came out, and I was already a huge Boba Fett fan before *The Empire Strikes Back* even came out. You know, he was the flipside to Han Solo. He had a jet pack, a cool ship, a really cool name. He was just always my favorite character."

The director of Chapter 14, "The Tragedy," endeavored to make Boba Fett's comeback memorable. "My approach was to pretend that this is the only other time or episode we'll even see Boba Fett. And it needs to satisfy – I don't want to take for granted that he'll show up again later in other episodes. This episode needed to say: 'Boba is back,' and that was my main personal mission."

To achieve this, Rodriguez went the extra mile and ended up "turning a three-page battle scene into a nine-minute battle scene." To show executive producer Jon Favreau what he had in mind, he even filmed a mockup

of Boba Fett's arrival in his backyard, using his children, dressed in Halloween costumes, as actors!

Actor Temuera Morrison, who played Jango Fett in *Star Wars: Attack of the Clones*, drew upon his Māori heritage to characterize Boba Fett's fighting style. Indeed, some of his moves were based on those of haka, a traditional dance that was often performed by Māori warriors.

According to property master Josh Roth, Morrison even requested a customized gaffi stick. "He wanted one that was longer and one that was more slender. If you look at the other ones from the earlier films, the shaft is just thicker and wider. It didn't lend itself to the choreography he wanted for this fight. We wanted to make sure we had something specific that he could use during the action scenes." Indeed, the fighting scenes where Boba Fett wields the stick were performed by Morrison himself, who had been trained to use a *taiaha*, a Māori staff, when he was young boy. ◗

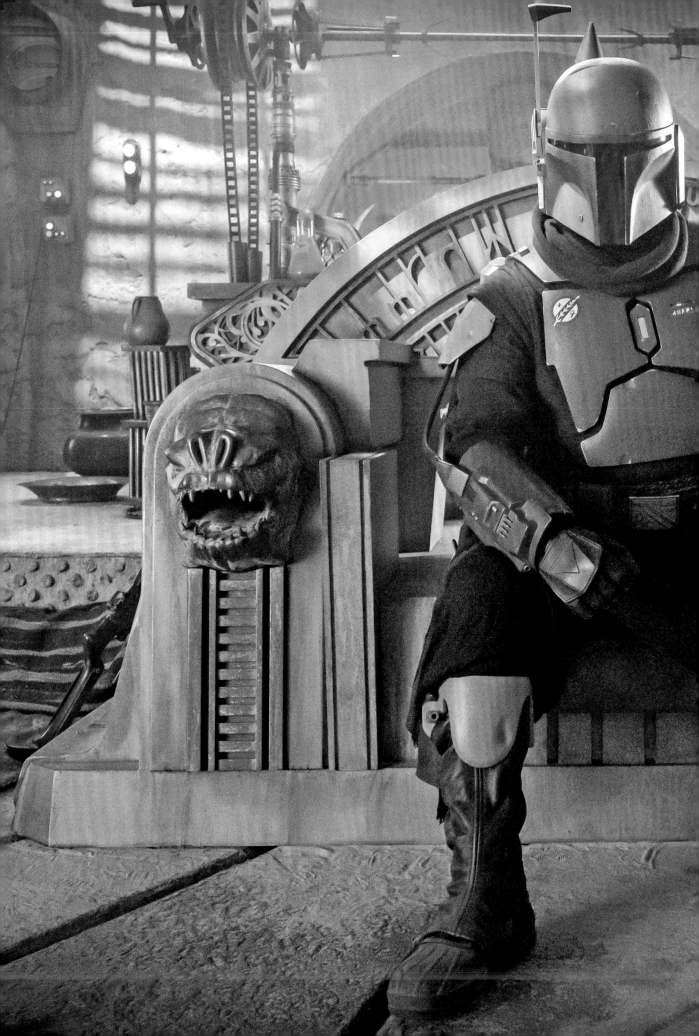

FENNEC SHAND

L eft for dead on the sandy dunes of Tatooine, Fennec Shand lives. Now in service of Boba Fett, who saved her life, the elite mercenary is willing to put her sharp eye and excellent aim at the disposal of Fett and whoever he is in debt to.

KILLER QUEEN

With her impressive list of clients, including crime lords such as the Hutts, Fennec Shand made a name for herself as one of the best mercenaries in the criminal underworld. Once the New Republic began to arrest many of her employers, Fennec went on the run and eventually hid on the planet Tatooine. There she was hunted down by aspiring bounty hunter Toro Calican, who enlisted Mando's help in capturing her.

While Djarin was temporarily away to find transportation, Shand tried to persuade Calican to free her and gang up on the Mandalorian, who had an even higher bounty on his head. However, afraid that she would kill him once released, Calican shot Fennec in the stomach and abandoned her in the desert.

Everything seemed lost for elite assassin Fennec Shand – until a mysterious hooded figure came to her rescue in the Dune Sea...

1 /

1 / Fennec Shand's bounty puck was originally picked up by rookie Toro Calican.

2 / Grateful to Boba Fett for saving her life, former elite mercenary Fennec Shand now works in his service.

A NEW EMPLOYER

The hooded figure turned out to be Boba Fett, who managed to save Shand by having her injured organs replaced with cybernetic parts. Owing him her life, Shand took an oath to join Fett's service and follow him on his missions.

Fennec may have lost her physical integrity, but not her abilities as a sharpshooter. Endowed with sharp eyes and excellent aim, Fennec Shand rarely misses her targets. When unable to use her primary weapon, a modified MK sniper rifle, the former mercenary employs her cunning. For instance, during the conflict on Tython, Shand managed to knock out several stormtroopers at once by pushing a giant rock down a hill, thus crushing the troopers as well as their heavy repeating blaster cannon.

BEHIND THE SCENES

To portray Fennec Shand, actress Ming-Na Wen drew upon... the character's name. Indeed, the name Fennec hints at the fennec fox, an animal whose behavior inspired Wen's performance. "I started looking at videos of the fox; when she needs to fight and move, she bolts, she goes! There's a lot of energy when she has to do that." Unsurprisingly, one of the main colors of Shand's costume is orange, just like the fox's fur. This further inspired Wen as well as hair designer Maria Sandoval, who came up with a taillike braid for Fennec's hairdo.

If Shand's braids refer to the animal world, the character's helmet hints at the medieval one. Indeed, Fennec's headwear – designed by concept artist Brian Matyas – is based on the medieval helmets commonly used by mounted knights, though with additional feminine lines.

Of course, the helmet proved rather challenging to wear while shooting the battle scenes. However, this didn't stop Wen, who proudly performed many of her own stunts. "I love doing physical stuff," she said. "Every day we're running, we're jumping, we're... you know, parkouring up these rocky mountain peaks."

As a huge *Star Wars* fan, Wen was over the moon with Shand coming back as Boba Fett's partner. She also greatly appreciated the relationship between the two characters and praised the "dependency and respect that they have for each other." ◖

3 / A stormtrooper about to be blasted by Fennec's perfect aim.

4 / Fennec may have been gravely wounded, but she didn't lose her fierceness.

5 / Fennec Shand soars into the air with her modified MK sniper rifle.

6 / The orange in Fennec's uniform resembles the color of the fennec fox, the animal she is named after.

1 /

GREEF KARGA AND CARA DUNE

Former Guild agent Greef Karga and mercenary Cara Dune have reinvented themselves as magistrate and marshal of Nevarro. The two joined forces and managed to mop up the planet, except for an old Imperial base with which they could really use Mando's help...

A NEW JOB

Since he parted ways with Mando, Greef Karga has taken on a new job – and a new look, too. In fact, the former agent has abandoned his role within the Bounty Hunters Guild and currently works as Nevarro's magistrate.

2 /

With the help of Cara Dune, Karga has extensively improved things on Nevarro, which has indeed become, under his jurisdiction, a respectable, peaceful planet. Not only did he manage to get rid of almost all the "scum and villainy," but he even turned the old common house where outlaws and smugglers would talk business into a school.

Some things, however, never change, especially when it comes to Karga's nose for business. When Mando, on his way to Corvus, stopped on Nevarro for repairs, Karga and Dune asked him to help them take down an old Imperial base and free the planet once and for all. With the Imperial base gone, Nevarro could also become a trade anchor for the whole sector – a prospect Karga seems particularly interested in. And who better to help than, in Karga's own words, "the best in the parsec"?

As his new role entails a lot of clerical work, Greef Karga has also hired, as extra help, an old acquaintance of his: the Mythrol fugitive who was captured by Mando in one of his last missions for the Guild.

3 /

1 / Despite being "steeped in clerical work," Greef Karga is very happy with how things turned out on Nevarro.

2 / Former mercenary Cara Dune is quickly climbing the career ladder.

3 / Students don't seem particularly interested in the astrography class.

4

GOING LEGIT

At last, fierce Cara Dune no longer needs to "lay low." After years working as a mercenary, Dune joined Greef Karga as Nevarro's marshal and helped him clean up the planet. Highly praised for her efforts, she was later recruited by Captain Carson Teva, a New Republic officer, who explained that the government needed local support to keep the Outer Rim under control. Initially reluctant, Cara Dune accepted the offer and became a marshal of the New Republic. Thanks to her role, Dune achieved a new level of authority – for instance, she now has access to a database that contains information about the New Republic's prisoners. She can also remand inmates to her custody and take them temporarily out of prison.

Dune doesn't like to abuse her power and is aware that her new position requires her to follow the rules. However, when it comes to helping a friend in need, she still strives to do as much as she can. When Mando asked her to spring Migs Mayfeld from prison, she eventually agreed to "pull some strings" to have him released.

4 / As a marshal of the New Republic, Cara Dune can help Djarin locate Migs Mayfeld.

5 / Djarin visits Nevarro's school. Concept art by Ryan Church.

6 / After "a bit of creative accounting," the Mythrol fugitive has resumed his work under Greef Karga to pay off his debt.

8 /

BEHIND THE SCENES

In addition to portraying Nevarro's bearded magistrate Greef Karga, actor Carl Weathers also directed Chapter 12, "The Siege," defined by director of photography Baz Idoine as a "rollicking adventure ride." "I think having that first season under our belts gave us a sense of the flow of the show, and the flow of the stories," said Weathers. "The more I got into it, the more I was able to sort of wear my actor hat when I'm in the scene and still be aware of, wherever the camera was set, what we were seeing."

A former professional American football player, Weathers starred in several action films. He has a deep understanding of how the action works, which proved particularly helpful when directing the twelfth episode. "That's something I've done in front of the camera forever. And then, of course, I was an athlete before that, so I know how it feels to get hit and I know how it feels when you're inside a scene, and it's moving and doing certain things."

Just like Weathers, former MMA (mixed martial arts) fighter Gina Carano is very familiar with the on-screen action. "Me and Carl speak a special language, I feel. We've both been action actors for a while, and I just think that he understands where I come from."

To reflect her new status as marshal, costume designer Shawna Trpcic slightly altered Cara Dune's armor. "I wanted her costume to reflect a higher station, a higher responsibility. So I upgraded her armor a little bit. I gave her a new paint job. It still has some cuts and bruises 'cause she's a tough dame, and I wanted to make sure I was respecting that as well."

Stunt coordinator Ryan Watson took advantage of Dune's upgraded role to show off her physical power. "She brings a lot to the table in terms of power. She kicks people, headbutts people, she does more of what she's good at." ◑

7 / Karga and Dune took advantage of Mando being around and immediately enlisted his help on a mission.

8 / Carl Weathers was also the director of Chapter 12.

9 / The New Republic marshal's badge given by Carson Teva to Dune.

9 /

MIGS MAYFELD

One thing is for sure: Migs Mayfeld certainly knows how to speak his mind. A former Imperial soldier, Mayfeld later joined a criminal crew of mercenaries and is currently serving 50 years in prison. An excellent triggerman, he has a sharp mind – and an even sharper tongue.

BECOMING INMATE 34667

Very little is known about Migs Mayfeld's past; indeed, he very much prefers to pick on others rather than opening up. According to criminal Ranzar "Ran" Malk, an old partner of Mando's, Mayfeld used to work for the Empire as a sharpshooter – not as a stormtrooper, as he likes to point out. After fighting in a war campaign known as Operation Cinder, Mayfeld left the Imperial Army and started working as a mercenary. He then joined Malk's criminal gang and took part, together with Mando, in an expedition to free a prisoner from a New Republic prison ship. There, Mayfeld and his crew attempted to betray the Mandalorian but were eventually captured by the New Republic, while Mando managed to get away safely.

Sentenced to 50 years of prison, Mayfeld was then taken to the Karthon Chop Fields to serve his time until one day, a New Republic marshal named Cara Dune gave him a new assignment...

2 /

1 / Inmate 34667, formerly known as Migs Mayfeld, wearing his prison uniform.

2 / Mayfeld and other inmates dismantle a wrecked TIE fighter in the Karthon Chop Fields.

JUST A SURVIVOR

3 / To Mayfeld, the New Republic is no different from the Empire.

4 / Valin Hess congratulates the alleged tank troopers on their successful delivery of rhydonium.

Underneath his cocky, arrogant attitude, Mayfeld hides a surprisingly human side. While fighting in the Imperial Army, the ex-sharpshooter witnessed the death of many innocent people, thus experiencing firsthand that, regardless of the team you're on, war always comes at a price.

Mayfeld is not proud of the things he had to do to survive; yet he also believes that "everybody's got their lines they don't cross until things get messy." Indeed, things got very messy in the Imperial mining hub on Morak when Mando and Mayfeld, disguised as Imperial troops, were forced to engage in conversation with Mayfeld's old commanding officer Valin Hess. When Hess stated that the thousands of soldiers and civilians who died during Operation Cinder were just a "small sacrifice for the greater good," Mayfeld shut him up – forever.

After managing to escape the Imperial hub, Mayfeld gave himself a last chance at redemption. As they flew away, he used Mando's cycler rifle to shoot a Juggernaut full of rhydonium so that Imperials could no longer use it. Impressed by Mayfeld's effort – as well as by his skillful shot – Marshal Dune eventually decided to set him free.

BEHIND THE SCENES

Quite curiously, actor and comedian Bill Burr, who plays Migs Mayfeld, has never been a *Star Wars* fan. However, when executive producer Jon Favreau told him there was a character he'd be a good fit for, he started to think about it. Eventually, Burr decided to accept Favreau's offer – a decision he also made thanks to his wife, who persuaded him to give *The Mandalorian* a go.

Burr particularly enjoyed working with Rick Famuyiwa, who directed both of the episodes his character is featured in (Chapter 6 and 15). As the actor explained "Rick has it all in his head. He's so cool and laid-back. If you watch the episodes that he's done, you think he'd be like this guy on his toes and really like that. He's just totally chill – the way he puts it together, it's amazing." ✪

5 /

6 /

5 / Director Rick Famuyiwa at work.

6 / Migs Mayfeld is once again a free man.

7 / Imperial Juggernaut. Concept art by Benjamin Last.

7 /

1

MOFF GIDEON

Unbeknownst to Mando, evil Moff Gideon survived. Alive and well, the ruthless Imperial is determined to seize Grogu back; this time, however, he can count on a new, terrifying army, as dark and powerful as the legendary weapon he fiercely weilds.

EVIL TO THE CORE

After surviving the crash of his TIE fighter, Moff Gideon resumed leadership of the Imperial remnant and went back to his primary mission: capturing Grogu and exploiting his "rare properties" to bring order back to the galaxy.

When it comes to, as fellow Imperial Valin Hess would say, "the greater good," Moff Gideon knows no friends or enemies. Indeed, he doesn't hesitate to kill his soldiers and allies if the situation so requires – or even worse, to make them die by their own hands. When, on Trask, Mando, Bo-Katan and the other Mandalorians managed to hijack an Imperial Gozanti freighter, Gideon commanded the ship's captain to crash the vessel with everyone inside it. While attempting to follow his master's orders, the captain was stopped by the Mandalorians. Having failed, he realized that Moff Gideon would never spare his life, and bit into an electrified pill that killed him.

As the powerful leader he is, Gideon has connections all over the galaxy and always "knows everything", thanks to his many sources. When Mando traveled to Nevarro for repairs, Greef Karga promptly ordered his workers to fix his ship. Little did he know that among his alleged "best men," there also was one of Gideon's spies...

Eager to capture Grogu to conduct mysterious experiments with his blood, Gideon managed to track down the *Razor Crest* on Tython. Once there, he deployed a squadron of dark troopers, which managed to kidnap the youngling and take him to Gideon's ship.

1 / Evil Moff Gideon lost Grogu once, but he's determined not to fail a second time.

3 /

THE DARK ARMY

Defined by Cara Dune as "a real skank in the scud pie," dark troopers are an elite infantry whose design has been extensively enhanced over time. Once soldiers in a heavily armored suit, they were eventually turned into advanced battle droids because, as explained by Dr. Pershing, "the human inside was the final weakness to be solved."

Employed by Moff Gideon's Imperial remnant, the third generation dark troopers are black-plated humanoid droids with red photoreceptors for eyes. Equipped with a blaster rifle and rocket boosters that allow them to fly, they are incredibly strong and can withstand extreme damage.

Designed to crush each and every opponent, Gideon's droids seem unstoppable – but everyone has an Achilles' heel, even in galaxies far, far away.

2 / Gideon's deadly platoon of dark troopers fly towards the temple ruins on Tython.

3 / As they draw much power, dark troopers cannot be kept at ready. However, they can be activated quickly.

4 / Moff Gideon shows the Darksaber to Djarin.

A BLACK-BLADED LEGEND

The keenest weapon in Moff Gideon's arsenal is also a legendary one: the Darksaber. Created by a Mandalorian Jedi known as Tarre Vizsla, the Darksaber is an ancient lightsaber with a dark energy blade. Throughout centuries, this unique weapon has changed hands many times, ending up, somehow, in those of Moff Gideon – and eventually in Mando's gauntlets after he defeated the Imperial in a duel.

An important symbol to all Mandalorians, the Darksaber must be won in battle by whoever aspires to become the leader of Mandalore. Indeed, when Djarin offered to give her the Darksaber, Bo-Katan Kryze firmly refused. For the Darksaber may not care who its wielder is – but "the story," as Moff Gideon sneeringly pointed out, is what matters.

BEHIND THE SCENES

A big fan of the early *Star Wars* movies, actor Giancarlo Esposito was particularly fascinated by the Sith Lord Darth Vader. "I thought that inside that very, very hard, coarse exterior," he explained, "could be a human being that had the ability to bring some light to our space odyssey in our galaxy."

Esposito spared no effort and performed all of his stunts in the second season. As Mandalorian double Lateef Crowder commented, "Giancarlo brings the greatest energy ever. It actually brings up my skill set, as well – if he's coming with a lot of energy and heart, I have to be really on point, too, and everything is going to look strong and on point. So, you know, we're literally fighting."

However, such great energy also resulted in many Darksabers getting harmed in the making of *The Mandalorian.* "We almost got into trouble by running through too many prop Darksabers," admitted the director of the season finale, Peyton Reed.

For the dark troopers the crew referenced their first appearance in the 1995 video game *Star Wars: Dark Forces.* Though they were portrayed by stunt actors, they couldn't look too human. As explained by visual effects supervisor Richard Bluff, "To really highlight the fact that there isn't a human inside the droid, what we're doing in visual effects is adding in all the pistons around the neck or the jointing around the elbows or the knees, the ankles or the shoulders." ◗

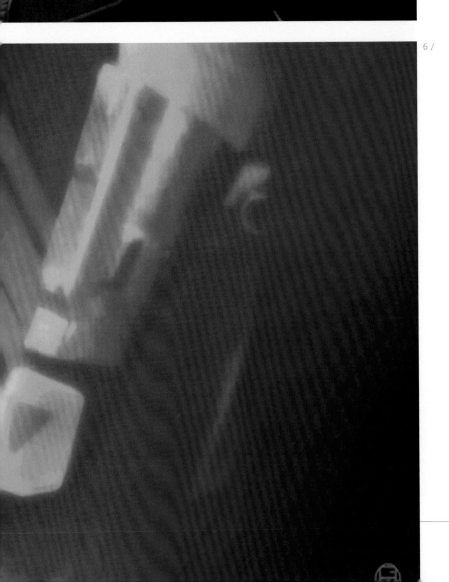

6 /

5 / Lucky for Mando, Gideon's Darksaber cannot cut through beskar steel.

6 / The evil Moff. Concept art by Brian Matyas.

7 / Next Spread: Concept designer Brian Matyas has defined his work with Gideon's costume, "one of the highlights" of his whole career.

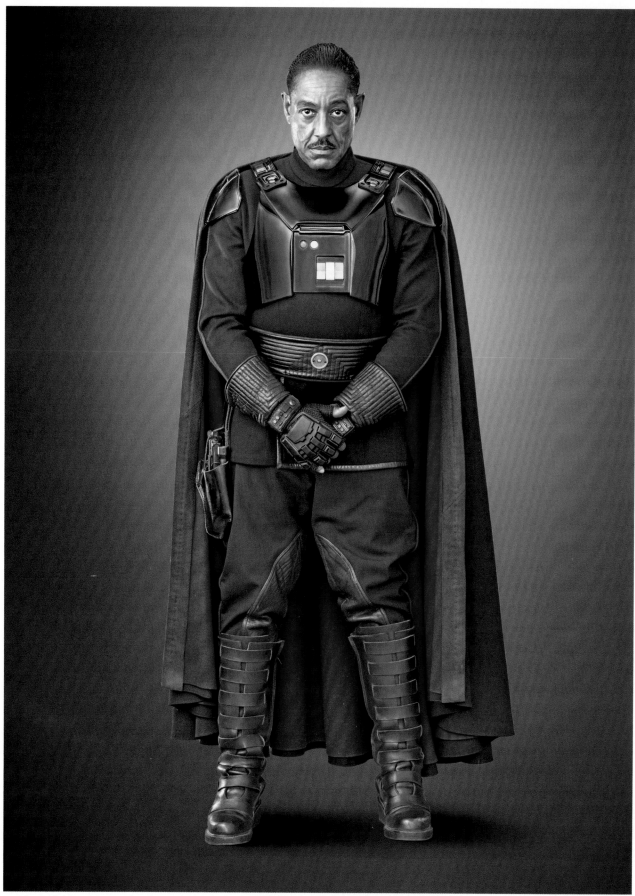

LUKE SKYWALKER

Luke Skywalker has once again saved the day. The legendary Jedi Knight is well-known across the galaxy for his role in the rebellion against the Empire. He is willing to train little Grogu in the ways of the Force – and who would be better suited for the job than Grand Master Yoda's former apprentice?

THE RISE OF THE FARM BOY

Before becoming a powerful Jedi, Luke Skywalker was just a simple farmhand living a humble – and quite dull – life.

The son of Jedi Knight Anakin Skywalker and Senator Padmé Amidala, Luke was born, together with his twin sister, Leia, during the rise of the Galactic Empire. After their mother died in childbirth and their father turned to the dark side, becoming Darth Vader, the newborns were separated and hidden for their safety. Luke was then taken to moisture farmers Owen and Beru Lars, relatives of his late grandmother, who raised him on Tatooine. Trying to protect their stepson, the Larses kept quiet about Luke's real origins and told him that his father was a navigator on a spice freighter and had died. Realizing that Luke had "too much of his father in him," Uncle Owen also strived to keep him busy on the farm, thus preventing him from leaving and putting himself in danger.

Chore after chore, Luke grew up wishing for a more adventurous life. An opportunity came up when Jedi Obi-Wan Kenobi asked Luke to join him on a mission to help the Rebel Alliance, a resistance movement whose aim was to restore democracy. Initially reluctant, Luke decided to follow Obi-Wan Kenobi upon realizing that the Empire had brutally killed his stepparents.

1 /

1 / Little Grogu marvels at Luke Skywalker's strength with the Force.
2 / The green-bladed lightsaber held by Luke Skywalker leaves no doubts about his affiliation.

3 /

4 /

3 / Luke Skywalker
makes his way through
the light cruiser.

4 / Skywalker uses
the Force to fight off
Gideon's dark troopers.

5 / Skywalker lost his
right hand in a battle
against Darth Vader.

Strong with the Force, Luke began training as a Jedi and received his father's lightsaber from Obi-Wan Kenobi, who had once been Anakin Skywalker's master before Anakin turned to evil. Thanks to the Force and his skills as a pilot, Luke Skywalker managed to help the Rebellion destroy the Empire's battle station, the Death Star, in a conflict known as the Battle of Yavin.

Luke then traveled to planet Dagobah and resumed his Jedi training under the guidance of Yoda, a legendary and powerful Jedi Master. Thanks to Yoda, young Luke Skywalker learned how to master his abilities and, most important, to believe in the Force.

Due to Yoda's death, Luke Skywalker couldn't complete his training. However, his journey to become a Jedi Knight concluded during the Battle of Endor, where Luke came to duel his own father – Sith Lord Darth Vader. After a strenuous battle, Luke prevailed but refused to succumb to his anger and kill Vader, proclaiming himself a Jedi, like his father before him.

Following the Empire's defeat and the birth of the New Republic, Luke Skywalker began to travel across the galaxy in search of knowledge that would help him restore the Jedi Order. But he also had another mission: to pass on what he had learned – thus fulfilling what Yoda asked him on his deathbed right before becoming one with the Force.

5 /

FULL OF SURPRISES

Though he couldn't complete his training, Jedi Master Luke Skywalker is incredibly powerful in the Force and can also count on exceptional lightsaber combat skills. After tracking Grogu to Moff Gideon's light cruiser, young Luke managed to defeat a whole platoon of dark troopers entirely on his own.

However, in addition to his Jedi weapon and Force-related abilities, Luke has another ally he can always rely on: astromech unit R2-D2! The blue-and-white three-legged droid has a very distinctive personality that makes him quite unique. Brave and selfless, he's always willing to lend a utility arm if his masters or friends are in need. R2-D2 is also very communicative and is not afraid to beep his feelings – like when he showed how excited he was to see little Grogu on Gideon's light cruiser.

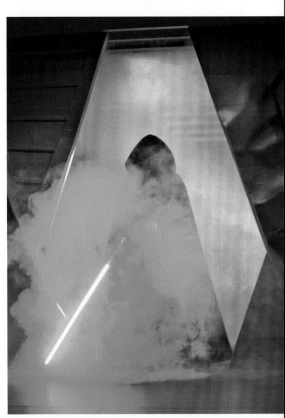

7 /

6 / A longtime friend of Luke Skywalker, R2-D2 is also a great fighter pilot's assistant.

7 / Hidden by a black cape, young Skywalker emerges from the shadows of Gideon's light cruiser.

BEHIND THE SCENES

To portray the son of Anakin Skywalker in the original saga, *Star Wars* creator George Lucas wanted somebody with a youthful appearance. From Robby Benson to William Katt and Charles Martin Smith, several well-known actors were considered for the part. However, after three weeks of unsuccessful research, Lucas and casting director Dianne Crittenden started to consider lesser-known actors, too.

In 1975, 24-year-old Mark Hamill was interviewed for the part. Initially dismissed, he was eventually offered the role after Lucas saw him interact with actor Harrison Ford, who was being considered for smuggler Han Solo. Indeed, the relationship between the two actors was very similar to that of their respective characters. In addition to this, Hamill has a somewhat innocent appeal that was perfect for portraying Luke Skywalker.

Mark Hamill was further involved in Luke Skywalker's cameo in the sixteenth chapter of *The Mandalorian*. Though physically portrayed by actor Max Lloyd-Jones, the legendary Jedi Master was still based on Hamill himself. Hamill was on set while the scenes were shot. As explained by visual effects supervisor Hal Hickel, "Mark had to be involved with crafting the performance. He was totally involved all the way through." ◊

8 / Skywalker has promised he will give his life to protect Grogu.

HUNTERS AND PREY

When one chooses to walk the Way of the Mandalore, one is bound to encounter all sorts of enemies – but a few trusted friends can also be found along the way.

1 /

COBB VANTH

Thanks to the Mandalorian armor acquired from Jawa scavengers, Cobb Vanth managed to buy his own freedom – and that of the town of Mos Pelgo. After liberating the city from the Mining Collective, Cobb Vanth became the town's marshal.

Since then, Vanth has been protecting Mos Pelgo from Sand People and bandits. But as tough as his armor may be, it's certainly not enough to defeat the massive creature that keeps spreading terror among the townsfolk…

1 / As the marshal of Mos Pelgo, Cobb Vanth doesn't take orders from anyone.

2 / The Frog Lady is looking for passage to the Kol Iben system.

3 / On top of being a skilled mechanic, Peli Motto is also, in her own words, "an excellent judge of character."

2 /

THE FROG LADY

The motherly creature known as the Frog Lady had to reunite with her husband on the estuary moon of Trask to have her spawn fertilized. Thanks to Mando, who gave her a ride aboard the *Razor Crest*, she managed to reach her husband in time and save her eggs – at least the ones she could keep away from Grogu's greedy hands.

PELI MOTTO

The operator of hangar 3-5 in the Mos Eisley Spaceport, Peli Motto may be a bit snappy at first, but underneath her rough mechanic's suit, she hides a kind heart. Years of working among species of "all shapes and sizes" have made Peli Motto quite proficient in several languages – a skill that comes in very handy when she has to find new players for sabacc.

3 /

DR. PERSHING

4 /Dr. Pershing is still conducting experiments for Moff Gideon.

5 /Morgan Elsbeth offers Mando a staff of pure beskar steel to kill Ahsoka Tano.

A skilled clone engineer, Dr. Pershing has continued to work for Gideon and the Imperial remnant. This time, however, he is determined not to disappoint the evil Moff again. In charge of the experiments conducted at the hidden laboratory on Nevarro, Dr. Pershing is a clever man but not a proud one. As such, when held at gunpoint, he's ready to leak even the most classified information.

MORGAN ELSBETH

The magistrate of the city of Calodan on planet Corvus, ruthless Morgan Elsbeth is still enraged by the death of her people, who were massacred during the Clone Wars. Ruthless and cruel, she rules Calodan by fear and intimidation. Plagued by Ahsoka Tano, who wants some information from her, Elsbeth hires the Mandalorian to get rid of the former Jedi once and for all.

VALIN HESS

A former general of the Imperial Army, Valin Hess works for an Imperial remnant operating on Morak. Coldhearted and merciless, he is not afraid to make unpleasant decisions – and sacrifice his own men – for the sake of the Empire. Hess strongly believes in his ideals and is determined to restore order to the galaxy – for order, in his opinion, is what everybody truly wants.

TUSKEN RAIDERS

As their other name, Sand People, suggests, Tusken Raiders are nomads who live in the most remote areas of Tatooine. They can be easily recognized by their heavy clothes, which protect them from the planet's suns, and the bandages they wrap around their heads. Fierce warriors, the Tatooine nomads often scavenge from moisture farms and local settlers. However, the sound of a krayt dragon is enough to send shivers down their cold-hearted spine.

6 /Valin Hess celebrates the Empire in what will be his last toast.

7 /Though they can be brutal, Tusken Raiders always keep their word.

ACROSS THE OUTSKIRTS OF SPACE

F ar from the Republic's reach, the Outer Rim planets are known to harbor a plethora of smugglers and scoundrels. These remote territories come in all shapes and sizes – as well as with all sorts of perils.

TRASK

The estuary moon of Trask orbits in the system of the gas giant Kol Iben.

To certain species, like the one the Frog Lady belongs to, Trask appears to be the only hospitable world in the galaxy. Indeed, the many oceans make it the perfect location for amphibious creatures, fishers and sailors. As explained by Bo-Katan Kryze, Trask has a black-market port often used by the Empire for the trade of weapons obtained with the plunders of other worlds. Its waters are also inhabited by a giant creature known as the mamacore, which has a mouth big enough to swallow Grogu's crib whole.

1 / A view of Trask's rippling oceans from space.

2 / Very little is left of Corvus's verdant forests.

CORVUS

Once a lush forest planet, Corvus's vegetation has been destroyed by the rage of Morgan Elsbeth. The ruthless magistrate has occupied the city of Calodan and oppressed its citizens, whose lives, in her own words, "means nothing" to her. Its barren lands and naked trees make Corvus a good hideout for Ahsoka Tano – as well as a good training ground for testing little Grogu's Force-related abilities.

2 /

3 /

MORAK

Unbeknownst to Mando, who strongly believes that "there is nothing on Morak," the planet is home to a secret mining hub. There, an Imperial remnant operates a refinery to process rhydonium, a highly volatile and combustible fuel. The planet is also inhabited by villagers who don't seem to be involved in political matters. As Migs Mayfeld bitterly commented, "Empire, New Republic. It's all the same to these people. Invaders on their land is all we are."

4 /

5 /

KARTHON

In the New Republic era, Karthon is the place where inmates are taken to serve their time. Indeed, Karthon is home to the Chop Fields – a correction facility where prisoners are commanded to take apart Imperial war machines that can no longer be used. Under the watchful eyes of security droids, Chop Fields inmates pass their time scrapping old Imperial "pieces of junk." Among them, Prisoner 34667, also known as Migs Mayfeld... ◑

3 / The planet Morak has a particularly warm climate.

4 / Boba Fett's starship lands in Morak's lush jungle.

5 / Apart from a New Republic correction facility full of wreckage, Karthon has very little to offer.

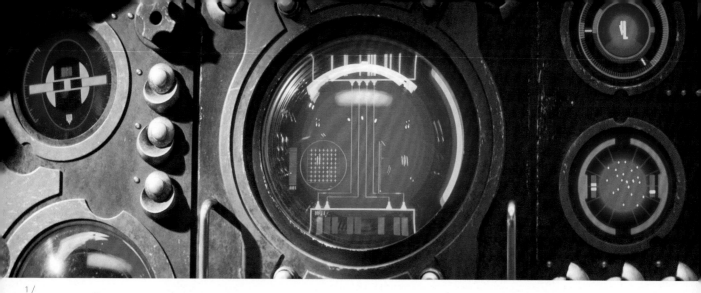

1 /

MOVING THE GALAXY

F rom woolly creatures to colossal warships, several means of transport encountered by Mando and Grogu during their quest. However, not all of them come with a removable control knob, much to Grogu's dismay.

BOBA FETT'S STARSHIP

Though it may look like an ordinary Firespray patrol ship, this legendary vessel is much more. Originally owned by Jango Fett, who had already added several features to the original model, the ship was inherited by his son Boba, who further customized it.

Feared across the galaxy, Fett's starship is packed with a wide array of weapons, many of which are hidden: twin rotating blaster cannons, a concealed turret with a tractor beam projector and two proton torpedo launchers, an ion cannon and a concussion missile launcher.

In addition to this, the ship comes with a sensor jammer that prevents the ship from being detected by scanning systems.

2 /

1 / "I have a lock": it's rather difficult to slip past Boba Fett's scanners.

2 / Just like his armor, Boba Fett's starship was previously owned by his father.

3 / To get rid of a few TIE fighters, Boba Fett launches a seismic charge from his starship.

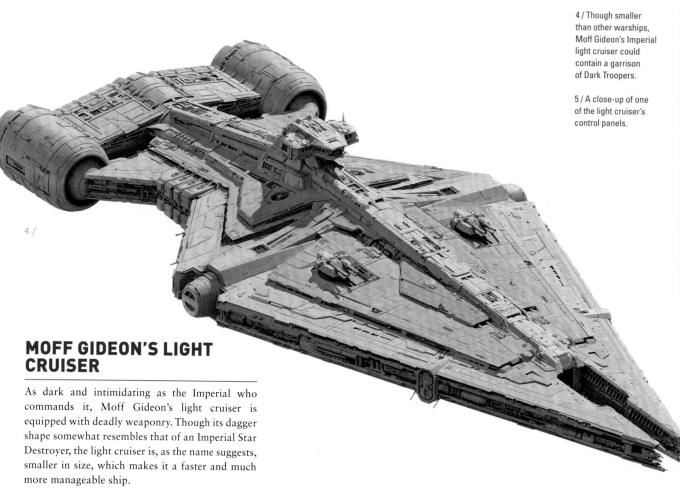

4 /

4 / Though smaller than other warships, Moff Gideon's Imperial light cruiser could contain a garrison of Dark Troopers.

5 / A close-up of one of the light cruiser's control panels.

MOFF GIDEON'S LIGHT CRUISER

As dark and intimidating as the Imperial who commands it, Moff Gideon's light cruiser is equipped with deadly weaponry. Though its dagger shape somewhat resembles that of an Imperial Star Destroyer, the light cruiser is, as the name suggests, smaller in size, which makes it a faster and much more manageable ship.

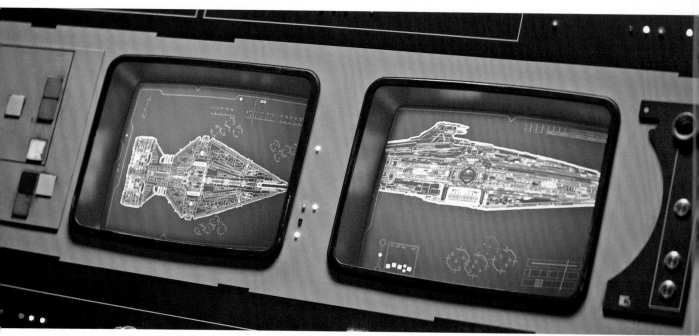

5 /

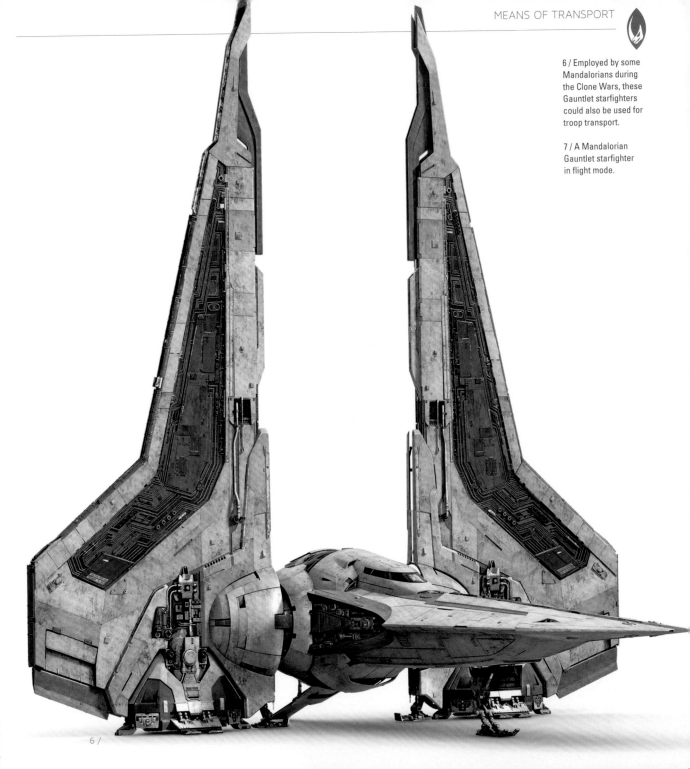

6 / Employed by some
Mandalorians during
the Clone Wars, these
Gauntlet starfighters
could also be used for
troop transport.

7 / A Mandalorian
Gauntlet starfighter
in flight mode.

6 /

MANDALORIAN GAUNTLET STARFIGHTER

The Gauntlet starfighter owned by Bo-Katan Kryze
and her allies is a combat ship and troop transport. The
ship's wings, which house the drive system, can rotate
separately from the primary hull. This feature makes
the quite bulky Gauntlet much more maneuverable.
The Gauntlet starfighter is armed with two pairs of
laser cannons, both forward and rear facing.

7 /

8 /

9 /

8 / Speeders come in
handy when traveling
across Tatooine's
Jundland Wastes.

9 / Cobb Vanth's speeder
is built on the engine of a
podracer.

COBB VANTH'S SPEEDER

Marshal of Mos Pelgo Cobb Vanth owns a rather
peculiar ride. His speeder, in fact, has been built with
the engine of an old podracer, to which Vanth has
added a rough flight control system and a saddle.
Despite its rather bizarre look, a speeder is still the
best vehicle for crossing Tatooine's deserts – however,
it may not be fast enough to escape from the terrifying
krayt dragon.

BANTHAS

Banthas are huge four-legged mammals covered in thick, shaggy fur. Despite their large spiraled horns, banthas are not aggressive creatures and can be easily domesticated. They live on desert planets, which explains why moisture farmers and Sand People often employ them for transport or companionship. ◖

10 / Unlike blurrgs, banthas are typically docile creatures.

11 / Over the years, banthas and Tusken Raiders have forged a deep bond.

STAR WARS LIBRARY

STAR WARS: THE EMPIRE STRIKES
BACK: THE 40TH ANNIVERSARY SPECIAL
EDITION

STAR WARS: THE MANDALORIAN
GUIDE TO SEASON ONE

STAR WARS INSIDER:
THE FICTION COLLECTION VOLUME 2

STAR WARS: THE SKYWALKER SAGA
THE OFFICIAL COLLECTOR'S EDITION

· *ROGUE ONE: A STAR WARS STORY*
THE OFFICIAL COLLECTOR'S EDITION
· *ROGUE ONE: A STAR WARS STORY*
THE OFFICIAL MISSION DEBRIEF
· *STAR WARS: THE LAST JEDI* THE OFFICIAL
COLLECTOR'S EDITION
· *STAR WARS: THE LAST JEDI* THE OFFICIAL
MOVIE COMPANION
· *STAR WARS: THE LAST JEDI*
THE ULTIMATE GUIDE

· *SOLO: A STAR WARS STORY*
THE OFFICIAL COLLECTOR'S EDITION
· *SOLO: A STAR WARS STORY* THE
ULTIMATE GUIDE
· THE BEST OF *STAR WARS INSIDER* VOLUME 1
· THE BEST OF *STAR WARS INSIDER* VOLUME 2
· THE BEST OF *STAR WARS INSIDER* VOLUME 3
· THE BEST OF *STAR WARS INSIDER* VOLUME 4
· *STAR WARS*: LORDS OF THE SITH
· *STAR WARS*: HEROES OF THE FORCE

· *STAR WARS*: ICONS OF THE GALAXY
· *STAR WARS*: THE SAGA BEGINS
· *STAR WARS* THE ORIGINAL TRILOGY
· *STAR WARS*: ROGUES, SCOUNDRELS
AND BOUNTY HUNTERS
· *STAR WARS*: CREATURES, ALIENS, AND DROIDS
· *STAR WARS: THE RISE OF SKYWALKER* THE
OFFICIAL COLLECTOR'S EDITION
· *STAR WARS: THE MANDALORIAN*:
GUIDE TO SEASON ONE

· *STAR WARS: THE EMPIRE STRIKES BACK*
THE 40TH ANNIVERSARY SPECIAL EDITION
· *STAR WARS: AGE OF RESISTANCE*
THE OFFICIAL COLLECTORS' EDITION
· *STAR WARS: THE SKYWALKER SAGA*
THE OFFICIAL COLLECTOR'S EDITION
· *STAR WARS INSIDER: FICTION COLLECTION*
VOLUME 1
· *STAR WARS INSIDER: FICTION COLLECTION*
VOLUME 2

MARVEL STUDIOS LIBRARY

MOVIE SPECIALS
· MARVEL STUDIOS' *SPIDER-MAN FAR
FROM HOME*
· MARVEL STUDIOS' *ANT-MAN AND THE WASP*
· MARVEL STUDIOS' *AVENGERS: ENDGAME*
· MARVEL STUDIOS' *AVENGERS: INFINITY WAR*
· MARVEL STUDIOS' *BLACK PANTHER*
(COMPANION)
· MARVEL STUDIOS' *BLACK WIDOW*
· MARVEL STUDIOS' *CAPTAIN MARVEL*
· MARVEL STUDIOS: THE FIRST TEN YEARS
· MARVEL STUDIOS' *THOR: RAGNAROK*
· MARVEL STUDIOS' *AVENGERS: AN INSIDER'S
GUIDE TO THE AVENGERS' FILMS*

MARVEL STUDIOS' BLACK WIDOW:
THE OFFICIAL MOVIE SPECIAL

MARVEL STUDIOS' THE FALCON AND THE
WINTER SOLDIER: THE OFFICIAL MARVEL
STUDIOS COLLECTOR SPECIAL

MARVEL STUDIOS' WANDAVISION
THE OFFICIAL MARVEL STUDIOS
COLLECTOR SPECIAL

MARVEL LEGACY LIBRARY

MARVEL CLASSIC NOVELS
· **WOLVERINE** WEAPON X OMNIBUS
· **SPIDER-MAN** THE DARKEST HOURS OMNIBUS
· **SPIDER-MAN** THE VENOM FACTOR OMNIBUS
· **X-MEN AND THE AVENGERS**
GAMMA QUEST OMNIBUS
· **X-MEN** MUTANT EMPIRE OMNIBUS

NOVELS
· **MARVEL'S GUARDIANS OF THE GALAXY** NO
GUTS, NO GLORY
· **SPIDER-MAN** MILES MORALES WINGS OF FURY
· **MORBIUS** THE LIVING VAMPIRE: BLOOD TIES
· **ANT-MAN** NATURAL ENEMY
· **AVENGERS** EVERYBODY   WANTS TO RULE
THE WORLD
· **AVENGERS** INFINITY
· **BLACK PANTHER** WHO IS THE BLACK PANTHER?
· **CAPTAIN AMERICA** DARK DESIGNS
· **CAPTAIN MARVEL** LIBERATION RUN
· **CIVIL WAR**
· **DEADPOOL** PAWS
· **SPIDER-MAN** FOREVER YOUNG
· **SPIDER-MAN** KRAVEN'S LAST HUNT
· **THANOS** DEATH SENTENCE
· **VENOM** LETHAL PROTECTOR
· **X-MEN** DAYS OF FUTURE PAST

THE GUARDIANS OF THE GALAXY
THE ART OF THE GAME

MARVEL'S AVENGERS BLACK PANTHER:
WAR FOR WAKANDA:
THE ART OF THE EXPANSION

MARVEL'S CAPTAIN AMERICA:
THE FIRST 80 YEARS

MARVEL: THE FIRST
80 YEARS

· **X-MEN** THE DARK PHOENIX SAGA
· **SPIDER-MAN** HOSTILE TAKEOVER

ART BOOKS
· *THE GUARDIANS OF THE GALAXY*
THE ART OF THE GAME

· *MARVEL'S AVENGERS: BLACK PANTHER: WAR
FOR WAKANDA* THE ART OF THE EXPANSION
· *MARVEL'S SPIDER-MAN* MILES MORALES
THE ART OF THE GAME
· *MARVEL'S AVENGERS* THE ART OF THE GAME
· *MARVEL'S SPIDER-MAN* THE ART OF THE GAME

· MARVEL *CONTEST OF CHAMPIONS*
THE ART OF THE BATTLEREALM
· *SPIDER-MAN: INTO THE SPIDER-VERSE*
THE ART OF THE MOVIE
· *THE ART OF IRON MAN*
THE ART OF THE MOVIE